Mixtape

Brandi M Burkhead

Presentation by *BookLeaf Publishing*

Web: www.bookleafpub.com

E-mail: info@bookleafpub.com

ISBN: 9789358312539

First edition 2023

ACKNOWLEDGEMENT

First and foremost I would like to thank my Mom who always made time to listen, critique, and encourage me. She's been my biggest fan since I found words. To Krys, thank you for being my editing eye and catching the typo I always manage to miss! The cover art you created for this book is fantastic, I'll pay you in coffee. I hope we never run out of projects to do together. My thanks to James, my big sister who peer pressured me into this project. To Asia, my first sister and the first member of my fan club, I hope I make you proud. My gorgeous, loud, dynamic, crazy family, thank you for always being a source of inspiration and encouragement. Words fail me when it comes to my love for you. Finally, to anyone who has listened to or read my work and encouraged me to keep going…my eternal gratitude.

Part of She

She is a part of me
Better than I'll ever be
And I am a part of she

In the flick of a wrist
A tilt of the chin
In maverick
In moxie
In fierce
In loyal
In tears of laughter
And cries of need
When the bough breaks
And happily ever after
All our favorite mistakes
And the give she can't take
In our children's kisses
And our mothers eyes
Hello hugs
I love you waves
A baby born
And our brothers grave
Finished sentences
And finished cups
Spilled tea

Coffee black
Shot of vodka — soda back
Crowded tables
Tuesday presents
Prom hair
Wedding dresses
From what God takes
To what he blesses...

She is a part of me
Better than I'll ever be
And I am a part of she.

For my Sisters

Pieces of Me

I'm goofy
And clumsy
And afraid of the dark
I'm bat-shit-crazy
Hate to think inside the box
And can come up with a quote for anything.
I can reason anything
logic little
And name all the presidents in order.
I want to be in love in the movies
Own a red velvet couch
And make the perfect cherry pie.
I'm obsessed with fashion magazines
French films
The history of the British Monarchy
Novel novels
And music you feel in your bones.
I dig 2am conversations
Shared cups of coffee
Hushed giggles
Stolen sleep
Art Deco
Videos of people tripping
And anything purple.
I find salad wedges

Cruiser cups
Crocks
And water pillows ridiculous.
I hate toast sweat
Vacuuming
The way 'sincerely' is spelled
And the smell of dust.
Someday I'll learn to be a grown up
Use commas correctly
Go to bed at a reasonable hour
Quit singing so loud
And occasionally off key
Stop swearing
And maybe do my taxes before April 13
But until then
I'll love museums
Children's finger paintings
Dandelions
A good PB&J
And a good water fight.
I'll laugh too loud
Fake accents
Carry seven different lipglosses
Brag about my family
Wear big sunglasses
And look for life to love.

If

If I had it
All the silly things
Silly dreams
Space
The place
Between wide rule margins
And dreams
I sneer
And poke fun
At the things
That grow in tight buds
On withered vines
Crossed out lines
I shrug them off
Old hopes that don't
Fit
Don't sit
Well on the shoulders of
My soul.

They lay quietly in a
Sweet cottage
Tudor style
On half a mile
Big bay windows

Grown empty
Without black haired boys
Family noise
On two feet
Evenly
I stand not cooking
Baking
Making
Aching
For creation
Of my own
On loan
From a heavenly deity
Who sees me unfit
Childs sweaty head
Husbands arm
40 hour week
And sleep.

If I had it
Those dreams
These things
Would be it be for
Granted
Taken
Forsaken
Buried among
The nit-pick & car pool
Unscheduled stops

And t-ball
Or would I know
Would it show
I had it all?

In My Head

It's all in my head
I lay in my bed
Wondering
Would a little serotonin
Make me feel a little less alone
And
It's all in my head
My brittle bones
Bite
My skin
Till I want to crawl out
But there's no out
Of
All in my head
This wonderland of dread
Doubt
Regret
Shoulda
Coulda
Woulda if
I coulda just
Stop
Reverse
Pause
Breathe

Be still
But
After all
It's all in my head

Death's Door

I raised my hand and held my breath
and knocked upon the door of death
Death invited me in with a smile
handed me a cup & sat with me a while
"Well my dear, it's nice of you to visit me,
but you have a choice to make," said he.
"Just sip your tea, no need to rush
We've plenty of time and much to discuss."

My eyes got heavy and I nodded off to dream
When I awoke another sat with me,
his face the same as when I saw him last
Tears filled my eyes and I started to laugh.
His hug was still just as warm and tight
"Welcome granddaughter to the light."
We spoke as if he had never gone,
He laid out my choice, each pro and con.

Death took my hand and cleared his voice,
"It's time my dear to make your choice.
You may stay and enjoy all heaven has to give
or return to your broken body and live.
No one will blame you if you choose to stay,
it wasn't your fault that car was in the way.
But you've been sleeping days that number eight

so it's time now to choose your fate."
A tear slid down my cheek and I took a big
breath
Said goodbye and walked out the door of death.

I Dreamt

of ocean breezes
and fiery sunsets
of companionable silence
and clasped hands
of spring grass
and cloud watching
of tangled limbs
and sweaty skin
of soft breathing
and sleepy sighs
of summer suns
and heated glances
of crowded tables
and raucous laughter
of passion soaked eyes
and hungry mouths
of love songs
and long drives
of autumn air
and honeyed words
of slow walks and
side eyed glances
of a healed past
and a promised future
of falling snow

and twinkling stars
of forever
and me and you

Untitled

This song always makes me think of you
Visions of a blues club in slow motion
The feel of chilled whisky on my tongue
Moisture in the air and slow dancing
The smile that was only for you
Tucked in your pocket
Easy banter and comfortable silences
How soft you made me feel
And the heat
Oh the heat
It makes my chest tight to know
To know what we could have had
If you weren't so afraid.

Invitation

15

What if I asked you for a dance
A songs chance
Skip the drink and the dinner
Move straight to sinner
We'll ride the carousel up & down
Round and round
Spit in the face of fate
Until we're aces over eights

Daymare

in the morning
the monster that hunted me all night
hiding in the shadows
is but a dresser once more
a forgotten Easter basket atop
a faded sundress falling out of a drawer

there no longer lurks
the phantoms that stole sweet sleep
they hide behind the day
making me foolish in the light
while logic crafts justifications for
the ethereal shrieking in my mind at night

dragons advance at dusk
summoned by fresh scabs on the soul
fervent eyes reflect so brightly
in terror i refuse to know, to see
i am no shiny armored hero
wretchedness fills my bitten holes and i cease to
be

Out of Ink

Is it a sign that my pen has run out of ink?
Has my mind let go of the verbs that sustain my
soul?
I can't see through the fog in my brain to the
words.
The words that let me breathe.
Have conjunctions that hold my soul together
fallen apart?
Have the adjectives been released back into the
wild?
Paper has been my sanctuary.
The place where I understand and am
understood.
Are the nouns that defined me becoming vapor?
The punctuation of my world ceased to follow
rules?
No longer a demi god in a kingdom of pen
marks.
Madness made sense with scrawling script.
Is it a sign?
Has my blood run out of ink?

Ink Joy

I finished.
Something.
A full complete thought:
Beginning,
Middle,
End.
Scratches across misplaced
cursive.
Lines of blue
that I can feel my
breath in.
A shift in my script
as I start to sob…
For the loss of
my sister.
For the loss of
my brother.
The loss of two
great joys
that guide my pen.
I grieved for
their voices.
I grieved for
their arms.
And I am ashamed

to say that
I grieved for
their pride.
Tears can teach
and I have learned
that my source of ink
is not depleted by
their absence but
deepened in color by
richer emotion.
I have more to say,
not less.
They are present in
every comma
question mark,
exclamation point,
and period of my life.

For Madd & J.

Fitzgerald

I hear people say that their mind is a carnival.
A circus.
A maze.
An amusement park.
One friend said her mind was a barrel of
monkeys with ADHD riding around on bicycles.
Some of my favorite people's minds are libraries
of notebooks
filled with social commentary, Friends
references, sarcastic comments, and lists of their
lists.

My mind is a Jay Gatsby party.
We aren't talking about Robert Redford/Mia
Farrow Gatsby.
We're talking full on Leo & Luhrmann Gatsby.
That heavily accented,
champagne wielding,
tuxedo wearing "old sport" Gatsby.

Fringe dripped flappers with sleek bobs doing
the Charleston
as the twisting rhythms of jazz bounce off of
paneled mansion walls.

Couples spill onto white balconies and
manicured lawns of deep green grass
and floral arrangements in stone pots,
the cacophony of drunken laughter
and roused conversation trail after them like a
wedding veil.
Crystal ashtrays overflow with yesterdays
conversations.
The shattered bits of an Art Deco vase glitter
defiantly on the Turkish rug,
the remembrance of words wished forgotten.
A discordant chord of the grand piano sounds
as a brunette balances herself on the key board
and her kitten heels.
Dark corners and velvet drapes hide the debris
of first kisses,
broken promises,
and hastily straightened stockings.
Best friends,
boyfriends,
and bravado are built and broken.
The clack of billiard balls
and the clink of glasses toast
to competition and companions.
Smoke from cigarettes in long enamel holders
lit by silver lighters slither around
strangers,
lovers,
friends

and enemies,
wrapping them in a ribbon of tobacco scented
reverie.
Some celebrate.
Some commiserate.
And in a corner,
tucked in a club chair
worlds are created and destroyed
with weapons of pen and paper.
Narrated in a voice "full of money", old sport.

The Poet

Where do moments go?
The debris of memories
The bits unimportant
Except to the dreamer.

Smoke from a fire
Lint from a favorite sock
A thread from a sweater worn during a shared
nap
The scent of love making and rain
The taste of a perfect red strawberry
A baby's first laugh
Steam from a hot cup on a cold night
A swirl of burgundy in a wine glass
A forgotten cigarette in an amber ashtray
The trailing scent of a woman
A piece of plastic played with by a kitten
An echo of laughter in an empty room
The way a certain name feels on the tongue

Do they evaporate and remix in a fairytale ether?
Do they arrive at a dream factory to be
reproduced?
Are they refiltered by the lens of a poet
Rewritten on lines of blue in black

Why

Why is the sky blue
Where did mommy go
How do airplanes fly
Who makes rainbows
What does purple taste like
Where does the tooth fairy vacation
Does Santa like snow
Can we get ice cream
Are you proud of me

All the things you want to know
Factual
Fantastical
History
and lore.
But things get complicated as you grow
with all the things you want to know.

Where does hate come from
Why do those shouty people have signs
What does invade mean
Why don't people want my Aunties to be
married
Are we mad at the president
and why are we wearing masks

Shouldn't we like all colors
How come that boy can't be a girl
Why does medicine cost so much
Why can't all broken things be fixed

All the things you want to know
And all I can say,
sweet child, is
stay soft
be gentle
and never stop asking.

For all of my babies

Scribbles

This is not the piece I wanted to write
I had a few lines dashed in a notebook
I know I did
I open composition book after composition book
I know it's here
Little scribbles fill random pages
But not my own meandering thoughts
purposeful ones made by tiny hands
Scratches
Shapes
Doodles
Outlines of hands
First attempts at names
Little love notes from the past
Bits of love left between play dates
They remind me why I write
Why I love this life
I hope I never snatch a pen from
A tiny hand as they decorate a fresh page
That I never lose sight of
the beauty of wild marks on a clean sheet
And maybe someday those same hands
Will open a notebook
And bleed a bit of their souls
On pages of paper loved by little hands

For the Cousin Crew

Taste

Like the autumn rain
The Chinook wind
Hose water
And fresh paper

A little danger
Reckless
Restless
And home

Like your favorite song
The last word
Worn in jeans
And salted caramel

A little fear
Falling
Crawling
And adventure

Like an open book
The shades of purple
Alliteration
And your name.

Belief

Key of b-flat
DaVinci's paint circling the heat of a star
Flamingos
Platypus puggles
The smell of fresh mowed grass
A baby just after it's born
Coffee's flavor
Tart cherries
First kisses
Sunset colors
The moment when laughter becomes a harmony
Forgiveness
Being petty for petty's sake
Dior dresses
Making love
and screwing
Toddler tricks
The ocean air
True family
THAT
Is how I can believe in God

Some Days

Some days my bones
Splinter into my flesh
My sheets are too loud on my skin
The blankets too light to hold
My soul within

Some days my emotions
Are more raw than my nerves
My safe space is an empty grave
Of good intentions and broken spoons
I cannot save

Some days tiny synapses
Light a fire under my skin
My backbone is weaker than my doubt
Searching for the fight to fight when
I want out

Some days the burden
Of being this kind of burden
Ripped as easily as a page can tear
To waken each day straight into
The nightmare

Some days I am triggered

By things I like to love
Their music too soft on my spirit
The poetry too smooth, too kind
To hear it

Some days my brain
Makes salad of my words
Thoughts pause and hang mid air
Syntax is too broken English to even
Pretend to care

Some days there is no rest
For body or for soul
I finally lay me down to not sleep
Unable to catch my breath or even
To simply weep

Let's Go

You wanna go?
You wanna fight?
I may not win but fair warning…
I go down hard.

I wear my cape of bravado
Drape my heart upon my sleeve
My insecurities inside a wide smile
Anxiety the jewels of my crown
I'm diamond hard
A backbone forged by fire
Fear is my shield of steel
This trauma is my weapon
Careful, this tongue bites

You wanna go?
You wanna fight?
You might win
But I go down hard.

Loved One's Prayer

I hope you never get to finish your own coffee
        that someone always steals half your
cup
I hope that you can no longer stand on your feet
        that you learn to lean on someone else
I hope that you experience the grief of loss
        that forces you to know you've loved
I hope you choke on your words so hard
        that you say exactly what you mean
I hope that you get so hopelessly lost
        that you find where you need to be
I hope that every mirror shatters at your glance
        that you can see your own heart
I hope that your life has ordinary moments
        so that you experience everyday
miracles
I hope that you sob your soul dry
        that the salt heals your wounded spirit
I hope that you get your fingers burned
        that you will live a life of fire...wild and
untamed.

Nightmares

When I was a child
I feared many things

I was afraid of
the dark
missing the bus
being broke
my parents dying

I had nightmares of
being lost
burned alive
kidnappings
being broken into pieces

My mother would rub my back
and she would say
Everything is alright
There's nothing to fear
It's just your imagination
— and I'm right here

Now as an adult
I fear many things

I am afraid of
the unknown
missing out
losing value
that the weight of grief will crush me

I have nightmares of
losing my grip
being consumed
stolen love
my spirit being unable to hold my body together

Still my mother rubs my back
And she says
Everything is alright
I know there is much to fear
You can handle this
— and I'm right here

For Mama, obviously